HEART OF THE FATHER

-2-

-Rachel Wenke-

Heart of the Father 2
By Rachel Wenke
Copyright © 2015

National Library of Australia Cataloguing-in-Publication entry
Creator: Wenke, Rachel, author.
Title: Heart of the Father / Rachel Wenke.
ISBN: 9780994273406 (paperback)
Subjects: God--Fatherhood. Fatherhood (Christian theology), Children of God.
Dewey Number: 231.1

Printed and bound in Australia in association with
Pentecost Life Centre
PO Box 625
Helensvale, QLD AUSTRALIA 4212
www.facebook.com/heartofthefatherbook

Contents

Acknowledgements

First and foremost, I give all the glory to God the Father, His precious Son Jesus, and Holy Spirit. Words could never express how grateful I am for Your love and mercy. You truly are the greatest delight and treasure of my life! Thank you for giving me the words to write this book and the grace for it to be published.

I want to thank my amazing sister Sarah for your time in proofreading and editing this book. You radiate the love and joy of God and I am so blessed to be called your sister.

Thank you to Daniel Jurekie for your technical assistance with the book's cover design and production. Special thanks as well to my pastor Butrone Leyshon and everyone at my home church, Pentecost Life Centre, who has supported and encouraged me. I am so blessed to be able to fellowship with such a beautiful family of believers.

Lastly, I want to thank my parents, Stephen and Wendy. Thank you for your selfless generosity and unconditional love. You are a blessing from God whom I will always cherish in my heart.

Introduction

In the depth of the Father's heart is a passion for you that is far greater and more precious to Him than any desire you could ever imagine. He is closer to you than the air you breathe right now. We are simply not aware of His Presence because we allow ourselves to be more aware of other things. But what would happen if you turned aside from the busyness of your day; the cares of life which ensnare your heart, and sought to know who God truly is? What would happen if you allowed yourself wholeheartedly to dive into the depths of His heart without restraint? What would you discover? The reality is that despite the majesty and awe that surrounds God, He yearns for nothing more than to have a deeper relationship with you; a relationship that can only be found through His Son Jesus.

As you read the words of this book and the accompanying Scriptures, may you receive revelation by His Spirit of the intensity and passion of your Heavenly Father. Like the first *Heart of the Father* book, the messages that you read in this book didn't come from my imagination or my toiling and effort. Rather, the words came to my heart by the Holy Spirit as I was resting in God's presence, listening to His heart.

As you read each of the messages, take your time to let them sink into your heart by His Spirit, and allow them to ignite in you a holy hunger to want to know God the Father and His Son Jesus more deeply. The depths that you can journey into God's heart are limitless, for the wonders of His love and nature are infinite. Come now!

Right Before You

Revelation 3:20a (NIV)

"Here I am! I stand at the door and knock…"

If I were standing right in front of you now, what would you say to Me? What would you tell Me? What would you do? Would you tell Me that you love Me? Would you tell Me that I am the only One for you? Would you tell Me that you need Me? Would you say, "Thank you"? If My Son was standing right before you now, what would you say to Him?

My child, I AM standing right before you now, the invisible God, I AM right before you. You cannot see Me but I AM here. I AM right before you now.

And My Son, Jesus Christ, is right before you. He is looking straight into your eyes, staring right into your heart. He and I are looking into your heart right this moment and We are hungry for your affection. Our eyes want to see Our reflection in your heart. We want to see Our love returned to Us.

My Spirit will open the eyes of your heart so you perceive Our standing before you, so you can perceive Our Presence. Even if you do not feel it in your natural members, you can know that I

AM right before you. I AM standing in your midst and I AM looking into your heart.

What do I see right now in your heart? Are there worries and affliction? Is there terror or pride? Is there doubt and fear and sin? Or is there love for Me, desire for Me, and affection for Me, birthed by My Spirit? Which do you think I want to see? Which do you think I yearn for in you?

I want to see My love in you. Then I AM seeing what I created, for I created you in My image. I AM love, so too then will I be in you; My love in you as you abide in Me.

See also:

1 Samuel 16:7, Psalm 11:4; 139:7-10, Zephaniah 3:17, John 15:9, 1 John 4:8

All I Ever Wanted

Genesis 1:27, 31a

"So God created man in His own image; in the image of God He created him; male and female He created them...Then God saw everything that He had made, and indeed it was very good."

Do you know what I have only ever wanted? Do you know what was the only thing I have truly ever desired, far more than any other?

Before I created the earth, and it was Us - Father, Son, and Spirit, dwelling together, I longed for more. When I created the angelic beings, they were not enough; I wanted more. When I created light and darkness, it was wonderful and a delight to Me, but it was not all that I wanted, I wanted more. When I separated the sea and firmament, and made land and sea, and filled it with all the animals and all the birds in the air, and creatures in the sea, still I was not entirely satisfied.

I had created a beautiful earth, a planet of exquisite wonder and it was good and pleasing to Me, but it was not all that I ever wanted. I wanted more. It was only when I created you, man and woman, that My heart could truly rest and be satisfied. Only then could I truly be delighted. For you My child are My prize creation, you are all I have ever really wanted.

Creating you is all I ever really wanted. You were made in My image, to dwell with Me. To commune with Me. You My love, you My dove, are all and will only ever be, all that I truly want. It is you. Your company. Your heart. You are all I've ever wanted.

Will you live your life in response to Me, living as if I am all you have ever wanted? For then My creation is truly complete. For all I ever wanted was for you to only ever want Me too.

See also:

Job 38:4-9, Psalm 73:25-26, Song of Solomon 5:2b

You Cannot Mould Me

Isaiah 64:8

"But now, O LORD,
You are our Father;
We are the clay, and You our potter;
And all we are the work of Your hand."

I don't think My children see the intensity in Me. I don't think My children - My church, see the seriousness and greatness of My love; the unfathomable nature of Who I AM, that cannot be defined or contained. They see Me as what is comfortable for them. They put Me in a mould of how they think I should be. They do not want to be made uncomfortable or challenged. Moulds were made to make bronzed and gold idols, and moulds today are still only for idols. I break all moulds of who you think I AM.

I mould you, but you cannot mould Me. I fashion you according to My image, in the likeness of My Son, but you cannot fashion Me according to the image of who you think I AM. I AM the Potter, you are the clay. I am not the clay waiting to be moulded by you.

How so many in My church have it wrong! They mould their church according to the comfort and needs and desires of their selfish ambitions, and then expect Me to fit their mould! You cannot assume or predict what way I will go or how I will move. I do not follow patterns- I break them! I do not conform to expectations- I exceed them!

I AM so much bigger than you could ever think or know. So much bigger than what your mind can mould Me into.

You fit into My mould but even the mould I have for you is not what you expect. You can never even mould yourself because you do not know the best way to fashion yourself. Only I know this. The mould I have for you is in the exact image of My Son Jesus and I will spend your lifetime perfecting you into His image. But you are a unique design that I hand crafted, and the way that I perfect you and mould you into His image is perfectly unique, unlike any other.

Stop trying to mould Me into your image and instead allow Me to mould you into Mine.

See also:

Psalm 139:5-6, John 3:8,
Romans 8:29-30; 9:20-21;11:33-34.

Furious Love

Hebrews 10:31

"It is a fearful thing to fall into the hands of the living God."

I don't think you understand the rage that is within Me. I don't think you understand the fire that is within My being. I don't think you understand the power that is built up inside of Me. I don't think you understand the magnitude of My fury.

I don't think you understand the anger I am allowing to be unleashed. I don't think you understand the devastation it is about to cause, the chaos about to erupt, and the disasters that will strike.

Because if you did, you would not toy with sin as you do. Because if you did - you would not take the impurity in your life so lightly, so frivolously. You would not be so flippant in your thinking, so flippant in your life, so flippant in your affairs.

Nobody truly comprehends how serious I AM when it comes to those I love, My children. Yes I AM love. And with all that I AM, I treasure you and I fight for you. But I AM serious about My love for you. I AM serious about how much I treasure you. I AM serious in My avenging for you. I AM not flippant in My love for you. I AM not flippant when it comes to fighting for you and My Kingdom. I am not flippant and I can never be towards you.

My love for you is fierce and it is piercing. Don't get in the way of My love for you. Don't come between Me and My love for you. Do not put Me to the test.

So don't put Me in a box and think that I do not unleash rage anymore because you think that this is not who I AM. You don't know who I AM. You can only ever know a glimpse of Me. You don't know what I was thinking or feeling a million times a million years ago before the earth was ever formed. You cannot begin to imagine what I was feeling or thinking when I watched My only beloved Son die for you. You don't know the manifold thoughts and feelings and plans that I simultaneously express and execute across the earth. You do not even know what I AM thinking or feeling right this moment in relation to your circumstances, unless I reveal it to you by My Spirit. So how can you think that you can predict what I will do or not do? What makes you think you can assume anything that I have not revealed to you?

The moment you begin to assume Me or My nature, is the moment you will begin to fall into error. All you must know is that when you put your trust in Me and draw your strength from Me, I will not fail you and you will know Me for all eternity. You do not need to know how or when or why I do things, all you need to do is trust Me. For My ways are higher than your ways, and will lead you into victory if you stay surrendered to My Spirit.

You see, My fury will never be unleashed on you when you are abiding in My heart. You will never see My fury when you are one with Me. I only unleash My fury on what is outside My heart and coming between Me and My Kingdom.

This is why I long so deeply for you to stay in My heart, to stay close and be one with Me, because I do not want you to see My fury. I do not want to fight against you. I want you to fight with Me, for Me, and I for you. Stay in My heart, abiding in the pleasures of My love always and this will be your experience. This will be your home.

Your home is a sanctuary in My heart. Outside of My heart is chaos and disaster waiting to happen. In My mercy, I allow you more time to return to Me without significant consequence, but I do not want you to test My mercy. I want you home where you belong in My heart, with Me. Time is running out. Come inside My heart and stay in there for this is the only place where I know you will not experience the unleashing of My wrath! Stay close to Me!

See also:

John 15:4, Romans 9:22-29; 11:22

Am I Enough For You?

Psalm 73:25

"Whom have I in heaven but You? And there is none upon earth that I desire besides You."

My child, right now, am I enough for you? Have I stopped your roving, wandering eye? Is the world still alluring to you? Is the incredible depth of My love for you not enough?

Every time you look for satisfaction in the world, every time you search for answers, for breakthroughs in the world to free you from your despair, to give you relief, you are telling Me that I am not enough for you. You are telling Me that what My Son Jesus did, giving His life for you so you may be free from sin and all darkness, is not enough for you. You are believing a lie.

You see My child, I AM always more than enough for you, so much more than you will ever need. My love and grace is more than enough to sustain and satisfy you. I will fill you to overflowing upon overflowing with My love if you let Me; if you yield to My Spirit. Why then do you think I am not enough? Why then do you act as if what My Son did for you is not enough? Why are you still looking to the world for your answer? Why do you want to work for your solution, to meddle and try and fix things yourself? Why will you not trust Me, that I have it taken care of? It is because you do not know Me, for My children who know Me are satisfied and know that I AM their portion. I AM their sufficiency. I AM their supply for all their needs. I AM their Provider. I AM their Rock. I am their Deliverer. I AM their Strength, and I AM always more than enough.

See also:

Psalm 18:2; 73:26, Isaiah 26:4, John 1:16,
2 Corinthians 12:9, Ephesians 3:20

To the Backslider:
When Did You Get Too Busy
for Me?

Revelation 2:4-5

"Nevertheless I have this against you, that you have left your first love. Remember therefore from where you have fallen; repent and do the first works, or else I will come to you quickly and remove your lampstand from its place—unless you repent."

When did you get too busy for Me? When did you get so preoccupied? At what point did I fade from being the centre of your heart, to the periphery of your cares? Do you remember at what point there was a shift? Do you remember at what point spending time with Me became a monotonous ritual to you, whereas before I was the Delight and Light of your soul? At what point was this shift? Do you remember? I do.

I remember the precise second in time when your heart began to shift. When your heart began to harden towards Me. For this precise moment when your heart began to turn away, was the precise moment that My heart began to break. Others could not see it, for you were still keeping the façade of Christian living, but your heart was beginning to tear away from Mine. I remember the turning point when all of a sudden I took second place; then third, then fourth. Then I was even hopeful to get a single thought My way from you. Your thoughts towards Me now are so sparse. How did this happen? How did this come to be, when once I was in the forefront of your mind?

I know how this happened. You stopped believing. You stopped trusting. You became impatient. You didn't see My word being manifested around you in the timing you wanted it to, so you stopped believing. You believed I existed, you believed in My Son but your heart stopped trusting Me and started to trust something or someone more than Me. You trusted your own judgment over Mine because you wanted your own way over Mine.

When you allowed this lack of trust to enter your heart, your heart towards Me began to harden. The more you began to trust in what was not of Me, the harder your heart became. I sent ones to help you. Those ones who were praying for you, but you resisted My word unto you. You continued to harden your heart.

You rationalise in your mind your current state of sin. But there is no rationale for what you are doing in My eyes. All I see is devastation when you are separated from Me.

But there is still hope for you. Never think that I do not desire you; that I do not love you. I love you just as much now as I did the day when you first surrendered your heart to Me. I adore you. I treasure you and I want you. My child, how I long for you! How I yearn for you! What are you doing? What are you doing wandering in the desert away from Me, when you could be basking in an oasis of the fullness of My love and mercy?

I want you back in My arms, My beloved. I want you back in My arms. No sin is too great that it cannot be washed away by the blood of My Son. Come to Me now, My precious child. Come back to Me now. I AM waiting.

See also:

Isaiah 1:18-20, Luke 15:18-24.

Your Avenger

Exodus 14:14 (NIV)

"The Lord will fight for you; you need only to be still."

Do you know that I delight to fight for you? Do you know that I delight to exalt you above your enemies and to seat you in high places above all calamity and darkness?

I AM your Avenger. I AM your Warrior, fighting for you. With the same passion that I love you, is the same passion through which I fight for you. And I AM not like any warrior – I already have the victory. The war has already been won! You are now the victor!

I want to fight for you, but you do not let Me. Why do you fight for yourself when I, Who already have victory, want to avenge you? Do you think your battle is too big for Me? Do you think your difficulty is too great? I have overcome death and fought all the armies of hell and won. No enemy or difficulty is ever too great to be a threat to Me, and no enemy or difficulty is ever too great to be a threat to you when you put your total trust in Me, for I AM your Avenger.

Let Me be your Avenger. Put down your rusty sword and let Me be your Shield, your Fortress, your mighty Warrior. Give your battles to Me and My victory will be yours.

See also:

2 Chronicles 20:17, Isaiah 41:2-4; 10-14,
John 16:33; 1 Corinthians 15:57,
2 Corinthians 2:14a

How I Show My Love

1 John 4:9

"In this the love of God was manifested toward us, that God has sent His only begotten Son into the world, that we might live through Him."

So many of My children beg Me to show My love for them. They ask Me, "Father, I want to know Your love, let me see Your love." My answer remains the same. Look at My Son Jesus. He is My love for you. The death and resurrection of My Son demonstrated My love for you, and continues to demonstrate My love for you today.

You see My child, you were once an orphan of the world, without a Father. Before you were born, I saw you in the future and I said, "I want you in My family, I love you; I choose you". I knew that I could not have you close to Me because of the fall of Adam. So I chose to give My Son Jesus- My only Son who I also cherished with all of My heart and loved as Myself. I allowed Him to be publicly tortured and suffer greater pain and humiliation than you could ever know, so that you would no longer be an orphan but could come into My arms and be close to Me.

Because of how greatly I love you, I gave up My Son for you. So when you tell Me that you do not know My love, you simply do not know what it meant when I gave My Son for you. My love was shown to you once and for all when I decided to give My Beloved Son Jesus for you. I separated Myself from Him so that you would never have to be separated from Me. He paid the ultimate price for you.

So don't tell Me that you cannot feel My love, don't tell Me that you cannot sense My love. My love is not a mere feeling, it is not a mere sensation. It is something you know in the depth of your being when you allow the death and resurrection of My Son Jesus to be real to you. My Spirit will make it real to you, ask Him now to show you, and He will fill you with the revelation of My deep love for you.

The cross is where My love was poured out for you. That is where My love is forever found- in the person of Jesus. His willingness and joy to die for you while you did not know Him reflects both His love for you and Mine. All the love you receive from Me is built on this.

See also:

Matthew 27:46, John 3:16, Romans 5:5, Ephesians 1:4-9, Colossians 1:12-14, 1 John 3:16

My Favourite Communication

Isaiah 29:13 (KJV)

"Wherefore the Lord said, Forasmuch as this people draw near me with their mouth, and with their lips do honour me, but have removed their heart far from me..."

Of all the forms of communication- My favourite, My most prized, is one that you cannot hear with your ears, read with your eyes or feel with your hands. It cannot be heard, seen or felt to the outside world; it is only known by you. What is this communication that I cherish so deeply? It is your communication to Me from your heart.

How I crave such sweet fellowship with you when you have rested your lips from moving, your mind from wandering and your body from exerting. Now you are just resting in My arms and your heart is knowing Mine. What this tells Me is far more than you could ever speak, act or declare with your lips. This is true love for Me; when you have ceased exerting your own efforts and entered My rest and you are beginning to hear My heartbeat. You are knowing My closeness, My Presence. Not words, not feelings, not outward signs, there is just stillness in Me and My stillness is beginning to penetrate into you. Communication is simply an exchange between two people. The greatest exchange I desire to have with you is outside of words, it is found in the secret place of your heart, resting deeply within Mine.

I love your praises and words unto Me when they come by My Spirit, but do not stop there with only words. Let's go beyond mere words. Let's go deeper together in our communication where no words can express. Come and enjoy My company without words and you will begin to sense My peace and Presence that no words can describe.

See also:

1 Samuel 16:7, Psalm 23:2; 42:7; 46:10,
Matthew 15:8, Mark 7:6

Resting Place

Matthew 11:28

"Come to Me, all you who labor and are heavy laden, and I will give you rest. "

When I speak to you, I do not seek to titillate your mind or body, but I speak to touch your heart. I want to speak to and connect with your heart. This is the greatest desire of Mine. How I long to penetrate through your logic, through your rationale, through your intellect, past your emotions, past your pre-conceived ideas and into the deepest part of you- your heart. I long to make My home in your heart by My Spirit. I long to find rest in your heart and dwell there, for only when I am at rest in your heart can you ever truly be at rest also.

I am looking for a resting place. My Spirit is looking right now for a resting place. Will you make your heart a home for Me? Am I welcome? The only way I am truly welcome in your heart is when you allow My Spirit to go past everything that attempts to stop Him from gaining entry.

What are these things which prevent My entry? The thoughts that tell you to turn aside to the world, the emotions that draw you away to cares and fears of the day; a stubborn will that refuses to let go of selfishness and pride. My Spirit cannot be at home in your heart, when there is also fear, anxiety and pride abiding there. You must lay these down to My Son, your Lord Jesus. Turn away from these things which weigh you down and turn to My Son Jesus, and as you do, He will take them away and in return give you rest for your soul. Your heart will be in total peace. This peace will intensify the longer you abide in this place of surrender.

I am looking for a resting place. Can I come into your heart now and rest in you? Can we be at rest together? The choice is yours.

See also:

Isaiah 26:3, Hebrews 4:1;9-10, Philippians 4:6-7, 1 Peter 5:7

The Allure of the World

1 John 2:15-17

"Do not love the world or the things in the world. If anyone loves the world, the love of the Father is not in him. For all that is in the world—the lust of the flesh, the lust of the eyes, and the pride of life—is not of the Father but is of the world. And the world is passing away, and the lust of it; but he who does the will of God abides forever."

One of the biggest lies Satan will weave in My children is that the world is more exciting than following Me, that the world and sin is more alluring. That to serve Me is to be a bore- a chore. These ones who fall for this lie have had the wool pulled over their eyes, for Mine is a Kingdom so fantastic, so intense, so perfect. But few ever see even a fraction of the depth of its splendour for they do not give Me the time of day, nor do they believe My words unto them.

But you see, My Kingdom does not appeal to your flesh, My Kingdom does not always appeal to your soul but know this My child: My Kingdom will always deeply satisfy your spirit. And when your spirit is satisfied, so will your soul be. When your spirit is not satisfied, so will your soul be restlessly craving for something that cannot be quenched.

If Satan ever lures you into thinking that what I have to offer is "boring" then you know that he is simply speaking to your soul and flesh. Therefore, if you are sensing this "boredom" you are simply listening with your old nature, not with your new man born of My Spirit. You see, your spirit man was made to worship Me. It was made to love and follow and serve Me and always be one with Me in righteousness and holiness. Your spirit relishes in nothing less.

Do you think heaven is a boring place? Do the magnificent descriptions of the heavenly creations, wonder and glory seem boring to you? You have no idea, My child! No idea! If you only knew the activity of heaven right now and what My saints are experiencing in the chambers of glory there, never would you think serving Me is boring. And My child- how I long to bring the atmosphere of heaven to earth through you, by My Spirit. But how can I release My glory in your midst when you are too busy being entertained with the falling vanities of this world?

When you are in the spirit, fellowshipping with Me your appetite will change. Do you know what you will find boring when you are communing with Me? The world; its systems, its government, its conversations, its entertainment - it will all seem frivolous and meaningless to you. The more you keep your eyes fixed on the glory and wonder of who I AM, and delight in Me and My Kingdom, watch and see the lustre of this world become more and more dull to you. Only what is of Me will truly inspire you.

While you are living in the world, you are to enjoy My creation, but you will see increasingly more the lack of meaning and depth within the world when it is without Me. Apart from Me, life and living is empty and hollow. But with Me, life is full of depth, riches, light and purpose. Life becomes inspiring, for My life is flowing through you!

The more you become inspired by Me, the more your life will inspire others and yourself. The more purpose you will have, for true purpose is only ever inspired by Me. If you look to the world and its vanity for your inspiration, do not be surprised that your soul fades into its greyness. Certainly, boredom and despondency will overcome you. Look to Me and you will shine My light. Look to Me and be inspired!

See also:

Psalm 65:4-8, Matthew 6:10, John 4:24, 1 Corinthians 2:12-14, Ephesians 4:21-24, Revelation 4:1-11

My Dreams and Desires for You

Psalm 139:16

"Your eyes saw my substance, being yet unformed.
And in Your book they all were written,
The days fashioned for me,
When as yet there were none of them."

I created you to dream and have desires, to aspire. You see, I too have dreams and desires, and you were made in My image. When I created you, I had specific dreams and desires for your life. I saw the end from the beginning of all that I desired to fulfil in and through you.

Looking at you now, I still hold those desires and dreams for you tightly in My heart, anticipating their fulfilment. But I gave you free will, so I will not force My dreams and desires to happen in spite of you. No, I want My desires to be your desires. My dreams to be your dreams. When My desire is your desire, then My desire will be fulfilled on earth as it is in heaven.

I have incredible desires and dreams to see you prospering, flourishing, and abounding in My grace, in every good work that I have set out for you, for the advancement of My Kingdom. But above all else, do you know what the greatest dream is that I have for you? It is that you would love Me as I love you. This is My greatest desire and plan for you- for you to love Me.

Will you fulfil the greatest dream and desire of My heart and love Me as I love you? Will you return the affections I have for you? Every moment, this is what I am longing for. This is the greatest desire I have for you- that you would draw nearer to Me by My Spirit and love Me with all your heart, soul and strength. Will you fulfil My greatest desire?

See also:

Psalm 21:2; 37:4, Matthew 22:37-38,
2 Corinthians 9:8

So Tender

Matthew 18:2-5

"Then Jesus called a little child to Him, set him in the midst of them, and said, 'Assuredly, I say to you, unless you are converted and become as little children, you will by no means enter the kingdom of heaven. Therefore whoever humbles himself as this little child is the greatest in the kingdom of heaven. Whoever receives one little child like this in My name receives Me.'"

I call you My child, not because I see you forever as a six year old but because I am your Father and I love you as My child, for that is who you are. The love I have for you is so gentle, so tender. How I long to protect you and surround you and keep you safe.

There is a softness in My love which I long for you to know. A gentleness and purity of My love which you will sense when you come to Me as a child.

Gentle does not mean weak. My strength is unmatched with any strength of the universe, for the entire universe is in Me. I can create or annihilate total planets and solar systems and slay armies and move mountains with My right hand's fingertip without any exertion. But do you know what is more powerful, and where I display most of My strength? The greatest display of My strength is shown in loving you. It is found when you receive the gentleness of My heart towards you. Knowing the tenderness of My love poured out to you by My Spirit through what My Son did just for you.

The more gentle and personal you sense My love and the more tender it makes you, the stronger you are actually knowing My love. For My love is not an impersonal wave or mist but a deep, deep, deep personal union with you, whereby you are clothed with a sense of belonging to Me. It is where wholeness, acceptance and peace begin to fill every layer of your being. How I long for you to experience even more of My tender love for you.

You can see My strength displayed in creation in My victory over My enemies, but My greatest feat of all is conquering your heart. If I do not have your heart, why conquer anything? My Son conquered all else - death, Satan, and sin, simply so I could have you.

My love is manifest more in My whispers than in My shouts. My love is known in gentle touches of My Spirit with yours, rather than in violent shakings. My love is known in the stillness of My Presence. Why do I want you to be still? Because My love towards you is so deeply soft and tender. To know the tenderness of My love, you must always keep your heart tender towards Me.

Let My Spirit keep you humble. Come as a child, come wanting to receive the tenderness of My love. There is a fight for your heart- a war, that wants your heart to be anything but tender towards Me. Do not let your heart harden towards Me so that you no longer sense My gentleness. Speak of My gentleness and tenderness to others and let them see My gentle goodness in you so that they may receive the tenderness of My heart for them.

See also:

Psalm 18:35, Isaiah 63:7, Matthew 19:14;
Mathew 23:37b, Colossians 2:10, Hebrews 4:7

What Makes Me Draw Near

James 4:8a

"Draw near to God and He will draw near to you."

How I long to draw nearer to you. To draw close to you. I am so in love with you. Yet I am also very patient. I never want to push Myself or force Myself upon you. I want to be invited, to be welcomed into your heart. Do you know what invites Me? Do you know when I feel most welcome? When your heart is dwelling upon Me. For then I will draw nearer to you. How this draws Me unto you when your heart is loving Me! I cannot help but come closer to you, to come nearer; and it is in these times when you will sense My closeness.

The more you love Me and dwell upon Me, the closer I will come to your awareness, for I am greatly drawn to you. Do you know how much I am already drawn to you without you even having to say or do a thing? I am so deeply drawn to your heart. Yet I refrain Myself from coming closer as to not come uninvited. And so I wait, watching and anticipating for the moment when you begin to draw unto Me with your heart. For then, at last I can begin to commune with you and fulfil the deepest desire of My heart!

You do not know what it does to Me when you sing to Me from the depth of your soul. You do not know what it does to Me when you love Me and give all that you are to Me. Oh how it draws Me! How it delights Me! How it draws Me when you are drawn after Me! Know always My precious and beautiful daughter, My precious son, I am and will always be so intensely drawn to you. But the question is, will you welcome My attention towards you by drawing unto Me?

You are an instrument of My delight and My pleasure. When you sing to Me, when you worship Me, when you serve Me out of love for Me, when you give all that you are from your love for Me, you are playing a beautiful melody to My heart. You do not know how much this delights Me, your Father! How I wish My children would not cease so quickly, how I wish they would linger longer in their love for Me.

You don't understand what it does to Me! You don't understand how it makes Me feel! If you did, you would never leave My face. You would never leave My embrace. If only you knew how much it draws Me unto you. Keep singing to Me! Keep worshipping Me! Keep loving Me! If you knew how strongly it draws Me- you would never stop!

See also:

2 Samuel 22:20b, Psalm 96:1-9; 104:33-34,
Isaiah 38:20, Colossians 3:16

Overflowing with My Promises

Hebrews 4:12a

"For the word of God is living and powerful..."

Do you know that every word that proceeds from My mouth is a promise? You can stake your whole life on a single promise I give you, for I AM forever faithful and true to My word! My word is who I AM and I cannot be unfaithful- it is impossible. I want to fill you with My promises. The more you are filled with My promises, the more they will flow out of you.

I want your life overflowing with My promises. This is simply a life that is filled with My word, My promises unto you. And as you are filled with My word, My word will overflow in your life. That is when you will see My promises manifest, when they can no longer be contained in you.

So don't ever doubt My promises if things appear as if My word is not coming to pass. It is not that I have forgotten you, it is that I am waiting for you to be filled more on My promises, on My word, so that they overflow out of you. Then My promises are fulfilled according to your faith in Me. I know when this will happen and can hasten it to My perfect timing and will for you by My grace and mercy. But more often than not, most of My children do not experience My promises. This is not because I

47

am unfaithful but because they do not fill themselves with My word, which is a living promise.

They do not fill themselves with My Son, My Spirit, who are living promises in you. You must see that every one of My words, My promises, is alive and wants to get out of you. They are bursting forth with life and want to be released and reproduce such life. They want to fulfil what I created them for in you.

Let Me fill you more with My promises, My child. Feed on My promises by feeding on My word; hunger for them and delight in them. Then, as you are feeding on My promises and are filled to overflowing, the overflow of My promise will manifest in and around you. The creative power of My word will have effect and accomplish its purpose in you.

What is it that I have promised you that you have not seen? Have you been filling yourself with My word and My promises in that area? Or have you instead focussed on the natural circumstances and lost hope in Me? Fill up, fill up, fill up, My child! Fill up on My word! Meditate on My promises, delight in them, and they will begin to overflow in and out of you for My glory! All of them which I have promised! For My word is FAITHFUL and TRUE. I AM faithful and true and everything that proceeds from My mouth will be done according to the riches in My Son Jesus.

See also:

Isaiah 55:11, Matthew 9:29, Hebrews 6:17-19,
Revelation 19:11

Your Thought Life

Proverbs 23:7a

"For as he thinks in his heart, so is he."

Your thought life is very important to Me. As a man thinks, so he is. Do not entertain temptations in your thinking. Do not dwell on potential traps of the enemy. Do not take the bait. So many children are taken hook, line and sinker through their thinking.

It starts with a thought. For every man that has ever fallen from the heights I called them to, it all started with a thought. A mighty devouring bushfire always begins with only a spark. As is your thinking. You must not kindle any thoughts which you know are contrary to My will. Do not imagine. Do not explore. Do not rationalise- put them to death! Think of Me and My promises for you. For every promise I have for you, Satan has a plan, often many plans, devised to see that the promises of Mine are not fulfilled.

Once you speak out My promises, watch and see Satan enter to attack the very thing that I am birthing. But do not fear his wiles. Do not retreat because of his ploys, you have nothing to fear, because I AM with you. All will work out when you know that I AM with you. I want you to guard your mind, be a steward of your thinking. Dwell on My house, My plans, My glory and majesty and Satan will find no entry point in you. His plans will be extinguished before they have a chance to catch alight.

Keep the fire of My Holy Spirit blazing in and through your thinking, and there will be no reason for you to dwell on anything not of Me. I am warning you of this, because of how precious you are to Me. Do not dwell on what you know is not of Me. When you entertain thoughts that have come to tempt you, you are making agreement with the enemy, for I never tempt you. Do not make agreement with a lie. Believe and dwell only on the truth, for in the lie is death but in My Truth is life!

See also:

Proverbs 4:23, Philippians 4:8-9,
2 Timothy 2:22, James 1:13

Time is Running Out

Isaiah 64:10-12a

"Your holy cities are a wilderness,
Zion is a wilderness,
Jerusalem a desolation.
Our holy and beautiful temple,
Where our fathers praised You,
Is burned up with fire;
And all our pleasant things are laid waste.
Will You restrain Yourself because of these things
O LORD?"

I look at the world. I look at My children, each of them one of My creation, and I see how much mercy I have poured out on them. How much restraint from My Judgment I have given them. But despite the mercy I forever grant the world, what does she do to Me? She despises Me. She mocks Me. She rejects Me. She curses Me. She objects and offers offence unto Me. She ignores Me. Yet generation after generation, I have kept loving her because I want more children with Me in My Kingdom. I want more sons and daughters to abide with Me. And so I give the world more mercy, more patience. But this cannot go on for all eternity. There is an end point to My mercy. A time where I say, "No more" "That is enough" and that time is soon at hand.

As much as it agonises Me to see the destruction of those whom I love and created, I AM a holy God and I have a plan for the earth which must be fulfilled. My Son Jesus is coming soon. He is returning to the earth in great power to fulfil My word spoken through My prophets. He is coming in glory and when He does, My elect shall be taken up with Him. But those who are not My sons and daughters, those who have lived for themselves in their revelry and rebellion against Me, those who exalted religion over Me, their self and possessions over Me, they will not be taken up. They shall see great calamity and death.

I do not want any one of My children to perish, I don't want it to happen but the time is coming where My Judgment will come upon the earth. Make sure you are not one who is left standing at My Judgment and told, "Away from Me you lover of lawlessness". Listen to Me now. Listen to your Father. There is a way out. A way of escape. Turn to the blood of Jesus. Turn to Jesus. Let Him wash away your sin and it will be washed forever from My memory. Now it is not too late for you, but then it will be. Do not hold off any longer. Do not hold off a moment or even a second from turning unto Me, for only I know the precise moment My Son Jesus is returning and believe Me it is very soon!

See also:

Psalm 103:12, Hosea 3:1, Matthew 7:22-23,
1 Thessalonians 5:1-10, 2 Thessalonians 2:5-9

Get Up!

Matthew 9:36-38

"But when He saw the multitudes, He was moved with compassion for them, because they were weary and scattered, like sheep having no shepherd. Then He said to His disciples, "The harvest truly is plentiful, but the laborers are few. Therefore pray the Lord of the harvest to send out laborers into His harvest."

You, who say you know Me. You, who say you are a believer. You, who come to church every Sunday and suppose to worship Me. Do you realise the multitude of souls who are about to fall into the lake of fire? Look around you! They are everywhere. They are in your workplaces. They are in your streets. They are in your family. I put you on the earth to have relationship with you; for you to know My heart and then for you to show My heart to others. But children, if you knew My heart, you would see that My heart is breaking for the lost! Yet, how few truly know My heart. How few there are who are willing to help Me bring the lost unto My bosom!

Where are they? Where are the ones who will forsake their self-interests and their fears and spread My word to the lost? Where are the ones who will rise up and demonstrate My love to those who are broken and needy? Where are they?

I am raising up an End Time army but many of those I wanted to recruit are deep asleep. They are in a slumber, a daze that I have not authored. What are they doing? They have followed traverses and streams but failed to follow the River of Life leading them to fulfil My will. They have been distracted and preoccupied with their own affairs and the deception of religion. Will you be the ones who will deny themselves and follow Me; who will follow My Son Jesus regardless of the cost?

All you must do is surrender to Me. Learn to hear My voice by My Holy Spirit and I will speak to you and lead you in how to lead others unto Me. It is not something you can do in your own strength. My Spirit will lead you and guide you in bringing the lost unto Me. But few even allow My Spirit to guide them in this way. Few give Him an ear. Seek My Spirit today. Enquire of Him how you, right this hour, can begin to harvest the souls around you who are hungry for the Living God, yet do not know how to turn to Me.

Get up from your slumber and open your eyes! Open your eyes and see as I see. See your fellow brother, your fellow worker, your fellow friend, how I see them. Open your eyes and see the love I have for them. The same love I have for you is the same love I have for them. Those who are not walking with Me are those that are walking into hell. Allow My Spirit to speak through you to these ones. Be My voice unto them. Intercede for them. Show them My love. Show them My Son Jesus. Do not stay in your slumber for a moment longer.

See also:

Isaiah 60:1-4, Matthew 7:13-14; 9:37-38
John 16:13, Ephesians 5:14-15, Revelation 3:1-3

My Lambs

Isaiah 53:7

"He was oppressed and He was afflicted, Yet He opened not His mouth; He was led as a lamb to the slaughter, And as a sheep before its shearers is silent, So He opened not His mouth."

Every day, so many of My lambs are being led to the slaughterhouse. They are being led to the slaughter and they don't even know it. My lambs are My children, My precious ones who I long for and want to nurture and keep close to My heart. But these little lambs have been scattered and wandered far from Me. I cry out to them, "Come home, come home to Me", but they are instead led by their sinful nature, and the love of this world. They do not realise that being led by anything or anyone but Me is the same as being led to a slaughterhouse.

I have already watched My Lamb, Jesus Christ, My Son, be led to the slaughter for your sin. He was slaughtered on the cross, before being raised again to life, so that you would not have to be. He did this so that the world could be free from the torture that awaits those in the eternal torment and darkness of hell. My Son's sacrifice paid the price for all. Because of Him I have plucked you from the slaughter that awaits you.

But My lambs do not see this, they trample on the holy blood of My Son and frolic in their sin. They are led by their worldly and carnal appetites, not knowing that this very frolicking will soon abruptly end for them. They are fattening themselves for the kill.

I do not want to repeatedly see My lambs being slaughtered. Tell My lambs of Jesus. Tell My lambs of who He is. Tell My lambs that His sacrifice is real but it must be lived in daily, through repentance. Don't let another lamb be slaughtered. One was enough for eternity. Tell My lambs now by My Spirit.

See also:

Genesis 22:8, Isaiah 40:11, John 1:29, Hebrews 10:29, 1 Peter 1:18-19; 2:25

The Great Storm

Job 36:27-33

"For He draws up drops of water,
Which distill as rain from the mist,
Which the clouds drop down
And pour abundantly on man.
Indeed, can anyone understand the spreading of
clouds,
The thunder from His canopy?
Look, He scatters His light upon it,
And covers the depths of the sea.
For by these He judges the peoples;
He gives food in abundance.
He covers His hands with lightning,
And commands it to strike.
His thunder declares it,
The cattle also, concerning the rising storm."

There is a great storm coming. A mighty storm brewing on the horizon. A storm that will destruct anything in its path. A storm of such intensity, that the devastation it will leave in its path will be unmatched. What is this storm? It is the storm of My glory invading the kingdom of darkness. Watch as this storm brings down princes and principalities to nothing! Watch as this storm turns Satan's plots on their head! I AM the storm that is coming to destruct anything not built on Me and I will not have mercy on those that have turned away from Me during this hour. My grace and mercy is new every morning but great tribulation is coming in this hour.

If you are not in the eye of the storm, that is in Me, you are in its path of destruction. Everything outside of Me is in the realm of the enemy for which My wrath is pouring out upon. Make way for My Spirit, follow My leading and knocking unto you and you will be safe from this destruction and devastation that is fast approaching. The clouds are getting darker, the sky is coming closer. Come in, come in. Watch My eye and stay looking at Me and you will be saved. Bring others unto My eye and they too will be saved.

See also:

Ezekiel 13: 13-14, Matthew 7:24-27,
Revelation 7:14-17

Do Not Restrain Me

Proverbs 1:33

"But whoever listens to me will dwell safely,
And will be secure, without fear of evil."

So many of My children say to Me, "That is enough. That is too far." They give Me freedom and liberty to a point and then they say, "Okay, that is enough". My child, this is not true freedom, for true freedom has no restraints! It has no borders! It has no restrictions. When you tell me "enough", what you are giving Me is contrived freedom in your life. You are still trying to control your life in your own strength.

How My Spirit yearns to express My ways, the ways of My Son Jesus through you, but how you will not let Him! How many times you tell Him, "No!" But I am saying, "Yes, My child!" You must stop this resistance. You must stop this resistance which is only rooted in fear.

Do you see what you miss out on every time you say, "No" to My Spirit? For if you did, your response would always be, "Yes." Your response would always be, "More Spirit, I want more!" Never again would you say, "That is enough" before I have even begun! You can never have enough of Me! I have not even begun to unleash My power and glory on this earth! The tip of the iceberg has barely even been revealed!

There is never too far for Me to go for I AM limitless. You must let go of these vain restrictions and borders that you put Me in, for I AM about to break them all and then some more! If you could only see the land I have already given you. But in order to reign in these new territories, you must let Me flow through you without restriction so I can lead you into what is already yours. You must let My Spirit flow out of you without interruption. Will you allow this?

Fear of man, doubt and insecurities all restrict My flow. Intellectual reasoning and natural thinking restrict Me. When you listen to these rather than Me, you restrain My outpouring, thinking that you are somehow keeping yourself 'safe'. You do not know what safe means. Complete safety comes the more you surrender to My care of you and allow Me to provide for you. This is safety. This is prosperity. This is abundance. When you restrain Me in your life, you are only restraining blessing and fullness; and embracing loss and curse.

Do not hold back what I have put in you, release it by the grace and power of My Spirit without restriction! Release what I have put in you, for it is Me! Release Me! And as I AM released, watch as all that I have stored up for you is released in and around you too.

See also:

Deuteronomy 1:8, Proverbs 8:32,
Matthew 16:24-26, 2 Corinthians 3:17

Pride

James 4:6

*"But He gives more grace. Therefore He says:
'God resists the proud, But gives grace to the
humble.'"*

Do you know what it is in your heart that
always says, "No" to Me? What it is that
opposes Me, by always seeking control of a
situation? What causes you to fear? What
causes you to doubt? What ultimately is the
greatest impedance to My flow in you? It is the
most vile thing to Me- pride. It began with the
fallen angel Lucifer and it is rampant in My
people today.

Pride seeks control always. It seeks preservation
of self. It seeks deliverance of self. It seeks
resolution of problems by selfish strength and
power. Humility in you seeks Me and My divine
provision flowing through you. Humility seeks
preservation through Me, deliverance and
victory through My Son Jesus Christ.

The most beautiful state a child of Mine can be
in is when I see them dependant on My
provision for them. When I see in their heart
that they have realised, "I cannot do this, I need
you, I want you". The reality is, many
unbelievers and the world can get through life
on this earth and even succeed according to the

world's standards without My provision. But they grieve My heart. If pride does not cause you destruction in this life, it most certainly will in the next and for all eternity if you do not turn from it.

Silent pride which goes on in the heart harbours an attitude that says to Me, "I can do this, I got it, I can control this" which is outside My provision and My sustenance. A child of Mine in pride will only call to Me when their own devices fail, failing to see that I wanted to be called upon from the very start. And more than that, I do not want to be just called upon in certain situations, I want to work with you and through you together by My Spirit, in fellowship with you, every step of the way in every area of your life. In no area of your life should you ever think that I am not needed.

You must see that I love to be included in every part of your life, I love to provide for you. But you will get to a place of maturity, where you will see that what I want more is to be wanted by you more than just being needed. I want you to use your will and cheerfully want Me to provide for you, rather than out of obligation or necessity. I want you to see My provision for you as something you cherish, something you love, something that is holy. I want you to cherish what I give you as you cherish Me.

Will you cherish and treasure My care and protection over you as you cherish My

Presence? When you do, then you will seek it. You will seek My touch in every area of your life and will not seek to taint things with your own desire to control. You will see that it truly is only I that can make all things good and it comes for those who love Me, those who want My care and delight in it. This is true humility and meekness. A heart that says, "Father, I want you to look after Me, as Your way is the greatest, for Your way is love." Truly blessed are the meek, for they will walk in their inheritance of My Kingdom.

I desire for you to want My help. Too many children only call on Me in a time of crisis when I want them to call on Me in the little things, in the details, for I want to help in all situations. This fosters in you an attitude of meekness and humility. If you think, "I can do this, I can handle this, but God you have to help Me only in the big things", then there is still pride residing in your heart. True humility allows me to provide in the big and the small, in times of hardship and in times of blessing. This is true humility.

When you allow Me to provide for you in times of blessing and joy, and still put your trust and dependence in Me, then I can trust you with even more. However if you only ever call out to Me in a crisis, I will come for you and deliver you but you will only end up in more calamities if every other area is still dependant on your own ability. There is only another calamity from the evil one waiting to strike in every area that is not dependant on My provision and care. For how can I give you My strength if you are not letting go of yours?

See also:

Psalm 37:11, Proverbs 16:18, Isaiah 29:19, Matthew 5:5, 1 Peter 5:5

Give Me Your Moments

Psalm 27:8

"When You said, "Seek My face,"
My heart said to You, "Your face, LORD, I will
seek."

My heart is always searching for a moment longer- a moment longer with you. A moment longer that I can spend holding you in My arms, you looking into My heart through My embrace. A moment longer where I can receive your love pouring into Me; the same love I gave you, returning to Me. A moment longer when your heart is one with Mine.

How I am longing for a moment longer where I am the centre of your focus, the centre of your attention. How I long for all eternity for a moment longer with you. How I design and orchestrate situations where I can spend just a moment longer with you- where you give Me a moment longer of your heart. Of course I want more than a moment, so much more. I want you to share all the moments of your life with Me.

I gave My Son Jesus for you for every moment of your life. But what do I get from so many of My children. All I get is fleeting moments. Brief, fleeting moments, few and far between, when I want all of them, I want all of you. I want all the moments of your heart to be with Me, to be abiding in Me. Every moment of every day, from now until all eternity. Give Me your moments.

Every moment I spend with you is so precious to Me. If only you could see how precious each moment I have with you truly is to Me.

I cannot force Myself upon you; only when you choose to be with Me, can I experience such moments with you. Please, let your heart linger longer in these moments when you are loving Me. Do not rush these moments, for they are what I hunger and desire, simple moments where it is just you looking upon Me and My Son. When you are loving Me. Give Me your moments. As you see how precious these moments are to Me, so they will begin to be more and more precious to you.

My Son died so that you could spend all your moments with Me. So that in all your moments, we could be together. He did not die for brief fleeting moments, few and far between. He died for every one of them from now and for all eternity. Let's live together, enjoying one beautiful moment to the next in love for one another! My Spirit will take you from one moment to the next, abiding in My Son Jesus and His Presence. You never have to leave! Every moment is precious, may every one be ours to share together.

See also:

Psalm 84:10; 139:16-17, Isaiah 43:4,
Hebrews 10:22

My Arms

Psalm 139:10

"Even there Your hand shall lead me, And Your right hand shall hold me."

Do you know that My arms are impenetrable? When you are in My arms, My embrace, nothing can touch you, nothing can harm you. The arrows of the enemy cannot penetrate you, for I AM your Shield.

Oh how I love to cover you with My arms and hide you away. How I love to wrap My very nature around who you are, so that all you sense around you is who I AM, My ways. I love to have this closeness with you! Not only are you in My hands My love, but know that during every situation which attempts to foil you, every circumstance which attempts to thwart you, I AM holding you.

In My arms, may you sense the strength of My hands and embrace, the might of My shield. In My arms, sense the warmth of My love which covers you. In My arms, sense the gentle guidance I give you, leading you unto one course and restraining you from another.

Do not move away from My embrace. Rest in My arms. Rest in My arms, for My arms are resting upon you

See also:

Psalm 3:3; 18:35; 91:1-7, Matthew 11:28

My Smile

Numbers 6:25 (NLT)

"May the LORD smile on you and be gracious to you."

Do you know that I love to see you smile. I made you so that when you smile, others too smile; for when you smile, you are in My image, for I AM always smiling at you My child.

When you are in Me, abiding in My Son, all you will ever see is Me smiling upon you. You light up My face every time you look at Me. My eyes cannot help but sparkle with joy, every time your eyes are set before Mine - for you are altogether wonderful to Me! You give Me as much joy as My Son Jesus gives Me, for I see you as I see Him. You radiate joy in My heart every time you look at Me and unto My Son.

Of course when you turn away from Me and leave My heart, then My smile will begin to fade. But the moment you turn your eyes back to Me, what grin you will see on Me!

He who abides in Me by My Spirit will laugh easily and smile much, for He who is in Me is like My Son Jesus and My Son loves to smile! And in My Presence is the fullness of joy! And why shouldn't we smile?! Death has been conquered! Satan is defeated! Victory is ours! I AM seated on the

Throne forevermore! And why shouldn't you smile?! Why shouldn't you laugh?! You have everything to smile about! You are seated in heavenly places with Me and My Son forevermore! Look to Me and let your laughter roar!

See also:

Job 5:22, 8:20-21, Psalm 16:11, Proverbs 31:25, 1 Corinthians 15:54-55, Ephesians 2:6

Love of Your Life

Matthew 10:39

"He who finds his life will lose it, and he who loses his life for My sake will find it."

 D o you know that I want to be the love of your life? Now and always. I want to be the One that you cherish most dearly in your heart. I want to be the One that you crave and desire more than anyone or anything on this earth. I want to be the love of your life. I want to be the reason that you wake up in the morning and the last thing you dwell on before you rest your eyes to sleep. I want to be the One for you, the only One. Will you let me be the love of your life? Can I be your song? Your strength? Your greatest delight? Will you let Me captivate the deepest part of your heart with Mine? Am I the love of your life? Can you truly say this to Me?

I want you to cling to Me so tightly with all that you are. I want your love and desire to always be for Me, your affection to always be upon Me. I want all of you. For this is simply My heart for you. You are the love of My life. You are My greatest desire. I long to cleave to you so tightly if you will let Me, and never let you go. You are the love of My life. Of all that is within Me, you have My greatest affection, you captivate Me

81

the most. You are the one for Me, as I AM the One for you.

Do you know what most people's greatest love is? For some it is their spouse, for others their children, or their possessions- houses, cars, or sports. But for most, the greatest love of their life is their self. Their need to preserve and sustain their self is what stops many from loving Me as their greatest love. The love of their life is simply themselves.

People think they must lose out in order to love Me, when the reality is they lose themselves but they find Me. And when they find Me, their greatest attention is no longer on promoting their self but coming closer to Me; not for their own sake but for Mine. Do you see? I want to be the greatest love of your life, not for your own gain but for Mine! Only My love can do this, for I love you not for My gain but for yours, so when you love Me in return- My love is complete in you.

You see, My love is more than just mere affection and endearment towards you. My love is the giving of Myself to you. My Son Jesus giving His life to you was the demonstration of Our love for you. Only when you give yourself fully to Me, do I really know that you love Me. True love gives itself entirely to the one it loves. I gave Myself all for you; will you give yourself completely to Me?

See also:

Psalm 73:25, Mark 12:30, John 3:16, 15:13-14,
1 John 3:16

Created for My Glory

Isaiah 43:7

"Everyone who is called by My name,
Whom I have created for My glory;
I have formed him, yes, I have made him."

Do you know that you were created for My glory? You were created for Me. For My purposes. You were created to know Me and to believe Me and to love Me. I fashioned you and designed you to fulfil My purposes for you. As a carpenter designs his workmanship for the purpose he desires, so I have designed you as My workmanship to fulfil exactly what I desire for you. Do not think that I have not equipped you to fulfil the function I set before you. For what builder builds a house that does not fulfil its original purpose? If even a builder knows how to design and create a house that fulfils its function, how much more do I know how to design and create you, as My prized creation, My prized possession, to gloriously fulfil your purpose.

You were born to know Me and this is who you are. You know My voice as My child. You hear My voice and only Mine. This is who you are. This is how I created you. You are holy. You are obedient to only Me. This is how you were made as a new creation. The problem with My children is they do not live in the new creation that I made them to be, so that they fulfil My purposes for them. Instead, they live from the old man which is already dead to Me.

Every layer of who you are is designed to love Me; to be all that I created you to be. Simply believe that this is who you are and you will fulfil My purposes for your life. You will bring much glory unto My name. When you embrace who I created you to be, you are embracing My heart.

See also:

Genesis 1:27, John 10:27, Romans 8:30, 2 Corinthians 5:17, Ephesians 2:10

Open Your Eyes to More

1 Corinthians 13:12

"For now we see in a mirror, dimly, but then face to face. Now I know in part, but then I shall know just as I also am known."

There is so much more to Me than the world ever sees of Me. Even those who are called and are My elect, walking with Me, still today see so dimly. They see such a fragmented view of who I AM. Of My Nature. Of My holiness. Of My Majesty. Of My ways. So dimly. I AM so much more than what your eyes can behold. There is so much more of Me to see. But what is stopping you from seeing more of Me? What is stopping you from experiencing more of who I AM and living in the more and the abundance that you behold in Me? It is your faith. It is your unbelief. You do not see more because your expectation of Me is limited. It is hedged in the confines of a mind that has not been continually renewed by My Spirit.

The church's view of Me is so obscured, so obstructed, so short-sighted. My children do not experience the fullness of My house and the rivers of My pleasure because they are satisfied with the dim view which they are beholding and there is no hunger in them for more.

If you want to see the more that is in Me; and believe Me, My child, there is so much more, more than you could ever begin to fathom; then you must seek the more in Me. Do not be satisfied or content with what you have. Rejoice in Me and delight in what I have shown of Myself to you, but always know there is more. I want you to hunger for this more.

There is so much more of Me! I AM the God of abundance. There is an abundance of glory, holiness, love, mercy, grace, wisdom, joy, peace, and righteousness in Me that is untouched simply because there is a lack of ones who are hungry enough to seek out the more that is in Me!

Do you want to know the more that is found within Me? Then seek the fullness of who I AM! Do not settle for lack, when you can have an overflow! Do not settle for mediocrity, when you can have abundance! There is more I want to give you, more I want to add to you, more I want to show you, but it all comes from Me. More cannot be added unto you, until you see it first in Me! Come and see the more that is in Me!

Come and see the fullness of My house! Come and live in that house and dwell and partake of the rivers of pleasure and delight that flow from within Me into you! What you have seen My child is only the beginning, what you have seen

My child is not even the surface of what I want to show you! Come and see the more in Me!

See also:

Psalm 5:7a; 36:8, John 10:10, Ephesians 1:3; 3:20

Your Invitation to
the Father's Heart

Your Invitation
to the Father's Heart

God the Father loves you with a love so strong that He sent His only Son Jesus to die for you, and be raised from the dead, so that you could have an intimate relationship with Him, for all eternity (John 3:16).

It doesn't matter if you have been to church your whole life or if this is the first time you have heard of God; the only way to have closeness with the Almighty Father and experience His love now and for all eternity is through His Son Jesus Christ.

Jesus is waiting for you now to surrender your life to Him by the power of the Holy Spirit so that you may experience the fullness of relationship with the Holy Trinity.

If you want to accept the Father's invitation and receive the person of Jesus Christ into your life, simply pray the following prayer with all your heart:

D*ear Heavenly Father,*

Thank you for sending your Son Jesus to earth to die and rise again for me so that I may know You.

I turn away from my sins and my old life and surrender my life completely to You now, Jesus. Come into my heart and cleanse me with Your precious blood. I receive Your forgiveness.

Jesus, You are now my Saviour and Lord. I belong to You - my heart is Yours forever. God Almighty, You are my Heavenly Father and I am Your child. I am now born again!

Fill me with Your Holy Spirit. I give You permission to have Your way in every area of my life. Help me to live every day so that I may please You alone.

In Jesus name I pray, Amen.

If you prayed this prayer with all your heart-congratulations! You have no idea the wonderful world that awaits you in the heart of the Father, through Jesus Christ!

The word of God says that we must confess our faith in Jesus (Romans 10:9). If you prayed this prayer, I encourage you to tell someone, preferably someone who also has a relationship with Jesus, about this eternal decision. Find a

Spirit-filled local church and start reading God's word, the Bible, to learn more about who God is.

The fact that you have accepted Jesus does not mean that your life will suddenly be without problems. The difference is that now, regardless of what circumstances you face, you can be confident that your Heavenly Father is with you and surrounds you with His love and protection. His Holy Spirit, your Helper, is ever present to help and lead you to victoriously overcome anything that opposes you, through the wondrous work of Jesus Christ.

Above all else, remember to always cherish your Heavenly Father and to love Him with all your heart, for He greatly, so greatly, treasures and loves you!

CPSIA information can be obtained
at www.ICGtesting.com
Printed in the USA
BVHW032036160622
639865BV00008B/1037